Drops of Pleasure

by Terri Bonin

Conroe, TX

www.JustaLittleDrop.com

© 2016 Terri Bonin

Cover by Angela Rose

TABLE OF CONTENTS

Drops of Pleasure

A Guide to Great Sex using Essential Oils

By Terri Bonin

Dear Reader,

Thank you for picking up this little guide. I wrote these words of encouragement and included recipes to use in the bedroom because it's my heart's desire to see more marriages make it to the finish line of "'til death do us part!" without murder being involved. Sex is a huge piece in the marriage puzzle, so keeping it AWESOME is a must. I address the wife throughout this manuscript because I'm not comfortable talking to a husband other than my own about sex, so if your husband decides to read it... fine... I don't have to know about it, right? I understand he might enjoy getting a woman's perspective on this topic, so let him read it if he wants to, but I wrote this book for you, wives, and I pray it catapults you from good sex to GREAT sex with your husband!

What to expect from this little guide: You will see how important sex is within the marriage relationship. I'll give you the reasons you WANT to have MORE sex. I'll read your mind and list your excuses. I'll help you overcome the anti-sex slump. And last, but not least, I'll give you tips to use essential oils to make things exciting and lubricant recipes void of chemicals and filled with therapeutic essential oils that will fill your senses with desire and cause you to chase your husband around the bed!

Disclosure: I can only safely recommend Young Living essential oils for the recipes provided at the back of this book for sexual activity. Only 2% of the essential oils produced on the earth are considered therapeutic, and Young Living is among the 2% with their Seed to Seal quality promise. Young Living's therapeutic grade essential oils are safe for the physical intimacy suggested in this book. Now, let's get down to business! (No pun intended. Really.)

Terri Bonin

Drops of Pleasure

Over Sexed?

What's the Big Deal about Sex?

Well, first, the world revolves around it! Literally! The world would cease to exist in about 100 years without sex, but it's more than that. It adds an element to life that we crave, an emotion that awakens us. Have you ever seen a James Bond movie with your husband? If not, there's a possibility you live in a hole or might be dead, so let's go with yes and continue. Would any of the 26 James Bond movies be as intense without the music? No! The music piles on excitement! Drums up anticipation! Stirs in extra thrills! Not relating? Let's try a more feminine example: *The Sound of Music*. What if *The Sound of Music* was changed to *A Story of a Large Family Escaping the Nazi's*... with NO MUSIC?! It would be closer to a dry documentary than a heartwarming story of love and survival. Movies would be dull without music. And a marriage without great sex is akin to a movie without music. Blah!

Marriage and sex go together like coffee and hot! Who wants lukewarm coffee each morning? Ugh! Give me hot!

Marriage and sex need each other like a bright sunny day needs a cool breeze to relieve the heat. All sun and no breeze make for a scorching experience. Throw a breeze into the air and the earth sings!

Do you get the point? An exciting sex life makes a marriage sweeter, but somehow the importance of it frequently gets lost in a marriage. Jennifer Flanders says, "Sex does for a marriage what good landscaping does for a house - it adds beauty and protects the foundation."

Think about the landscaping around your home. If you give it attention and love, then it blooms with beauty each season. Neglected landscaping becomes a pain in the neck because of the weeds, ant beds, and vines that need uprooting. A neglected tree within landscaping can actually break the foundation of a house! Sex within marriage IS similar to this landscaping. It needs consistent attention to bloom into full beauty and protect the foundation. Consistent is the key word in the above sentence. Sex is better when it's consistent. Keeping a ball rolling is easier than stopping and starting it.

If you don't love sex with your spouse, decide right now to change that! You CAN begin to love it, even crave it! I promise! You married each other, so there must be something in the relationship to work with. I say *start with sex!*

The other day I was pushing my toddler in a basket around Walmart and she asked (rather loudly I thought), "Mom, do you have superpowers?" Her question took me off guard. *What's this about? I thought. Superpowers? Me?*

She answered herself without missing a beat, "Dad says you do!"

Ha! The root of the question reveals itself. I'm glad he thinks so. I'll take that compliment any day! And the funny thing is I know *exactly* why he thinks I have superpowers.

Thank you very much.

You have superpowers, too. Forget the fact that your husband doesn't take out the trash or play with the kids. Those issues will resolve themselves in time if you have a healthy intimate life. It's supernatural how a regular time of intimacy with your spouse can override a multitude of daily irritations, sealing the foundation of a marriage! A wife who understands this is using her superpowers within her marriage. Use your superpowers!

As a young mom I never understood when older women would say, "The most important thing you can give your children is a happy marriage." Now that I have children who are old enough to recognize love in action, I get it. Kids grow in security when parents play with each other. It's become one of my goals to embarrass my kids by flirting with my husband. It's good for the whole family.

Kids get thoroughly embarrassed by mom: √.

Husband feels wanted and grows in confidence: √.

What keeps a couple from playing like this together more? Any answer to this question is an excuse. Flirt with your husband!

Anyone can pay the bills, cook the meals, play with the kids, mow the grass…you name it. But YOU, the wife, are the ONLY one who can kiss your husband all over his body while God smiles over you! You are the only one he can plant his seed inside with God's full blessing. Your body is the only woman's body your husband is allowed to admire fully naked. So don't cheat him of this pleasure! Be unashamed! He CHOSE you! You see imperfections, but he sees womanly beauty. Glory in it! Enjoy it! You expect him to be faithful to a monogamous sex life *with* you, therefore let him enjoy every aspect *of* you. You get to spend the rest of your life together figuring each other out. Study your man. Learn the skill. Drop your inhibitions. Get comfortable in your own skin. Give yourself freely to him with confidence.

Sometimes, in response to sex being used in unhealthy ways around us, we as women can hear the message that sex is bad or dirty. Like so many beautiful gifts given to us by God, sex is sometimes taken out of context and used in ways that God did not intend. However, if we miss the beauty of sex in its intended purpose, we miss out on a truly amazing gift that God provided to unite husband and wife in marriage as one flesh. A healthy sex life blesses a marriage.

I'm about to give you several simple essential oil recipes to enhance your sex life, but I want you to know upfront that these oils ENHANCE! If you want magic and healing in your marriage, then PLEASE read the books listed at the end. A $12 dollar book is SIGNIFICANTLY cheaper than private marriage counseling, which I DO think is necessary at times. But reading the books will put you years ahead of the game. Invest in your marriage in this way!

Not Tonight!

What if you're married and you don't like sex?

No problem. There's hope for you! First, let me list a few reasons you want to take the steps to learn to like sex. The health benefits are CRAZY!! Here's the short list:

Sex:

- Causes better sleep (It really does!)

- Tones muscles (Especially the core and booty)

- Gives a younger appearance (Because you're HAPPY!)

- Resets hormones (Yup!)

- Alleviates depression (Who doesn't feel lifted after being loved on?)

- Lowers blood pressure (Aerobic exercise helps lower blood pressure, as well as the hormone oxytocin, which is released during orgasm!)

- Is a pain reliever (No doubt! It relocates all mental energy away from the pain!)

- Increases immunity (Because when you're happy, you're immune system works better.)

- Lessons stress and anxiety (Who can be anxious in the arms of a husband?)

- Improves cognition (Who can think straight in a sexless relationship?)

- Increases circulation (Gets the blood pumping!)

- Burns calories (Even more when you do it right!)

- Reduces cravings (Because you're satisfied.)

And the list goes on….You can read a more comprehensive list with a detailed explanation and studies cited in the book *Love Your Husband/Love Yourself: Embracing God's Purpose for Passion in Marriage* by Jennifer Flanders. I HIGHLY recommend it!

Put the above list to the test. When you can't sleep, wake your husband! He won't mind, and it will be just a matter of minutes before you're sleeping too.

Got a backache? Great! Forget about it for a few minutes while you have an intimate time with your husband. It works. And the funny thing is, you'll want the relief the next night again!

Are you emotional, feel crazy? Been there. I'm typically emotionally stable… *sans pregnancy* and get this, I've been pregnant 101 months of our marriage.

take a moment of silence to ponder that number

That's approximately 8.4 solid years of emotional surges! That's a lot of craziness, but that's also a lot of physical intimacy because thankfully, my husband and I learned along our journey that sex resets the hormonal balance and makes me functional again. (Exit crazy momma!) It's magic. It's fun! Who would have thought?

Put the list to the test!!

Don't Touch Me!

If sex has so many health, benefits why don't we do it more?

Good question. These are the most common excuses:

Too tired!! - There are a number of reasons a person can be tired. Lack of sleep is the most obvious. Sleep is important. Schedule enough time for it. If falling asleep or staying asleep is a problem, then use essential oils to help! There are several sleepy oil choices. Try the oil blend Tranquil, or rub lavender and cedarwood on your temples and neck. Diffuse these oils next to your bed. Drink 2-4 drops of lavender. I drink about 4 drops on those nights I'm not tired but it's getting late. My husband drinks double the amount of lavender that I drink before bed. Vetiver is an AMAZING sleep oil, too. It is a low tone oil that will put you into a deep sleep and help you wake up fresh. My husband and I are oil junkies in the sleep department, but hey! It could be worse, right? Here's the sleepy oil list:

- Tranquil
- Lavender
- Cedarwood
- Vetiver
- Roman Chamomile
- Bergamont

- Marjoram

Next, work on your sleep rhythm. Sleep will pull on your eyelids at a decent hour if you make yourself roll out of bed earlier. At first this may mean you'll be dragging out of bed versus bouncing out of bed, but the healthy rhythm will come. Studies have proven that people who practice a regular sleep routine are trimmer and healthier than those who have sporadic or even late bedtimes. Think about it. Healthier weight, happier marriage because you're rested and more cheerful during the day...yes, the benefits of taking control of your sleeping habits are worth it! Forget about the weight benefit, your marriage is worth it. Most people need a solid 8 hours of sleep to feel rested. I know that's true for me and I bet it's true for you, too. Up your sleep game.

Besides sleep, vitamins, or lack thereof, can play a key role in your energy level. Personally, if I don't take my vitamins, I'm worthless. And I mean WORTHLESS! I call it being vitamin dependent. Some people are, and others aren't. I am. So I take supplements to keep this body moving. My top favorite supplements for energy are:

- Ningxia Red

- Master Formula

- Sulfurzyme

- Super B

I take a few more supplements for other issues besides energy that you can read about on my website (justalittledrop.com), but the ones listed above are the ones that give me the energy to function like a normal human. I also have a few favorite oils I inhale deeply if I need an energy boost. They are:

- EnRGee
- Endoflex
- Joy
- Inner Child
- Any citrus oil (lemon, lime, grapefruit, orange, citrus fresh)
- Mister (I actually rub this one on my wrists and neck and gain super powers from it! No kidding! Try it! I LOVE Mister! It's a game changer for me!)
- Valor I or II
- Grounding

My list of favorites may change next week, but those are the ones I keep in my purse today.

Overeating - When I spend the day mindlessly stuffing my face, the last thing I want to do is get naked and be touched!! If a full, bloated tummy inhibits you too, then understand that overeating actually becomes a selfish act against your spouse. Ouch! I know. Don't touch my food! It's one of my daily pleasures, but seriously consider pushing back the plate if it affects what happens under the covers with your spouse. However, understand that overeating can be caused by being nutrient deficient and take action. If you seriously struggle with overeating, then you need to supplement. Give your cells what they are screaming for and they will become satisfied with smaller amounts of food. If you do not give your cells what they need for fuel, then your will to NOT overeat will be in battle with your chemistry that is SCREAM-ING for nutrition. In the will versus chemistry battle, self-will rarely wins. Supplements that are infused with essential oils are absorbed into the cells regardless of the condition of the gut, so consider this when you're choosing your supplements. Another easy trick to tame the hunger monster is inhaling the essential oil peppermint. Studies have been conducted on peppermint and weight loss, and it was discovered that inhaling peppermint be-fore meals can help you push back the plate. The peppermint causes your hypothalamus to think your stomach is satisfied! Imagine that! It's strange, but it works.

Too busy - Some seasons are busier than others, and there is nothing we can do about it. But in too many instances, our cul-ture finds it socially acceptable for activities to destroy families, as if activities are the key factor in what makes or breaks our chil-dren! No!! Stop the insanity! Children need strong families more than they need little league. I know in my family, when our kids are too busy, our marriage is affected. My husband and I choose who plays sports in each season and he coaches their teams as much as possible to keep us connected. We control our nightly activities so that we can sit around the dinner table AT LEAST 3 times a week. It's proven that families who do this build stronger emotional bonds than families who don't. Guarding the evenings helps marriage and family! Don't get TOO busy!

Wounded feelings - Face it, we girls get our feeling hurt and ex-pect our men to figure out what's wrong on their own. That's just not fair. Men don't see the world through our sensitive eyes. Sex makes your husband putty in your hands and gives you the opportunity to tell him gently what's on your heart afterwards. Sex opens the door to clear communication. Benefit from it!

No desire - This is a pretty common one among women. You obviously WANT to WANT sex, but your hormones are against you! First, address your hormones. I suggest:

- Fem Gen
- Progessence Plus
- Prenolone Plus
- Sage
- Marjoram Clary Sage
- Dragon Time
- Mister
- Lady Sclareol
- Thyromin
- Ningxia Red
- Master Formula
- Super B
- Essentialzyme
- Life 5
- Omegagize

- Endoflex

- En-R-Gee

- Frankincense

You can learn more about these products in the Essential Oils Desk Reference, or at youngliving.com. Another fun tip that sets me in a happy mood is showering with essential oil body products. When I lather up with Dragontime shower gel and lotion my body with Sensation body lotion, I feel happy. My hormones love me when I shave with Mirah shave oil. Is it placebo or are the oils truly altering my mood? Who cares? It works!

Also, concerning your desire toward your husband, don't underestimate the power of prayer. I've been in that place with no desire, so I prayed about it. I KNOW God wants husbands and wives to enjoy this aspect of marriage often, so when I struggle, I take it to the One who designed the activity in the first place and He ALWAYS helps! In a nutshell, I ask my Creator to help my body to crave my husband's body, and I am proactive with my hormone oils, my thoughts, and my actions toward my husband. It works. Prayer always works. "...The effectual fervent prayer of a righteous man availeth much." James 5:16 KJV.

Yes. I'm telling you to pray about your sex life and ask God for His creative ideas in the bedroom. He'll surprise you. I promise.

Don't feel well - First, get a physical exam to make sure everything is ok. If all's well, but you are certain you're body is not right, then DEFINITELY begin to make changes. First, start drinking Ningxia Red DAILY!! It feeds the cells and will give you the fuel you need to move forward in other ways. The highly absorbable Master Formula multivitamin listed above will greatly help, too! My body LOVES that supplement pack. Also, the web has a TON of information on eating clean, so make sure you're eating real foods to nourish your body. If you don't feel great, it's hard to have GREAT sex, so consider everything that goes into and onto your body, including soaps, lotions, body care products, and candles. Everything we rub on our skin or inhale is absorbed into our bloodstream and affects our health either to strengthen it or weaken it, thus the reason I love using Young Living's body products. My cells love the them! Be intentional concerning the products you use so that you can feel your best!

Different bedtimes - In rare cases, different bedtimes cannot be avoided, but most of the time it's just sloppy scheduling. Get under the covers each night WITH your husband, because it's healing. It says, "You're more important than… (fill in the blank.)" Sit up and read together. Talk. Snuggle. Make bedtime your favorite time of day because of the quiet one-on-one time you get with your spouse.

Make it Happen

My husband and I were married 2 weeks before he started dental school, and we quickly became two ships passing in the night as our schedules began to steer in opposite directions. As poor college students trying to survive, it didn't take long for us to realize one of us needed to drop out of school if we wanted to eat. We like food. So I took the honor and landed a stable job downtown. In the evenings, with all my leftover energy (sarcasm intended) I ran a busy little home business. My new life partner attended school by day, studied in the evening, and threw the newspaper in the wee morning hours! We evolved into hardworking roommates trying to stay afloat with our bills and responsibilities. One evening, while sitting at our kitchen table with books and paperwork sprawled everywhere, my young husband looked at me and said, "We should have sex."

I literally opened my calendar, studied it for minute and answered with a yawn, "How's Tuesday night? I'm open."

Ridiculous!

It's funny now, but the point is, we had to PUT IT ON THE CALENDAR because we were both inescapably busy and EX-HAUSTED! During that season, when he was balancing dental school and working and I was juggling two jobs to help ends meet, we literally wrote "sex" on the calendar at least a few times a week (insert party horn). We wanted each other. *We wanted to want each other*, but we had almost every single excuse listed above standing against us. We chose to press into the situation and set our appointments for sex. I'm glad we did.

Fast forward several years and many kids later, my husband and I still enjoy a consistent sex life without having to yawn through the experience or set appointments. It's frequent and fun now that we've adjusted to the burdens of adulthood, but the fact is life did not slow down. Rather, it has a new set of challenging responsibilities, but we've developed the habit of pressing into our intimate life regardless of outside circumstances. Don't wait for life to slow down. It won't. We deem it a priority because physical intimacy within a marriage heals soul wounds and emotionally bonds a couple. But don't let me fool you, just because we have a nice rhythm does not mean we're always on the same page. For instance, one Saturday while working around the house we decided we needed a break from our chores. I understood that we were sneaking away for a quick lunch date and would return home right afterward we ate. However, after lunch he pulled the car up to the Marriott! In his mind, he had planned the ultimate surprise for me!! I was surprised all right when I understood his intentions. I was MORTIFIED! My hair was greasy. I had on my least favorite EVERYTHING! I had the legs of Conan the Barbarian! Was I happy about this surprise trip? NO!! Call me spoiled, but I like to be prepared, clean, feeling pretty... We talked through how I felt, and since then we have put "Marriott" on the calendar! Some women are ALWAYS prepared for this type of surprise, but I'm not one of them. Half the time I have spit up on my shirt and peanut butter in my hair. Thus the life of a mom of many, but I wouldn't trade it! I love my life, my kids and my husband's high sex drive. I just like a little heads up before clothes start flying.

If you find yourself in a similar situation, get with your husband and write "sex" on the calendar with him. The anticipation will give you both a swing in your step. You'll make sure your legs (and appropriate body parts) are freshly shaven. (Try the Mirah shave oil! MmmmmmMmmmm!!) You'll have on your favorite panties (maybe some lingerie to get you in the mood, some crotchless panties, or perhaps none at all 😉). You'll have your essential oil mixtures easily accessible, and your mind will be in the game! There's something to say for budgeting physical intimacy into the schedule!! Plan it. And make it happen!

Bring it On!

Action Steps - Before the Oil!

Good sex starts in the brain. Yep! Let me prove it. Don't you find it hard to get naked with your husband when he's ticked you off and you're mulling it around in your head? Of course you do! It's impossible to give and receive tender caresses to the one you're seething over! Your brain is furious, and your body revolts against him. Ok! Assume you're over it. You've kissed and made up. A happy truce saved the day. Now you're enjoying a fun time of intimacy with your man and all of the sudden you remember a project deadline due TOMORROW! **BAM**! All those happy, warm feelings JET! They book a plane to Mexico and flee your body! Good sex starts and *is controlled by your brain!*

Prepare your brain. Forget your "To Do" list. Forgive your husband. Decide you want a happy marriage. It all starts here. Make the choice to give and receive kind words and gestures throughout the day. This is where so many marriages fail. A little irritation begrudges a couple from actively pursuing kindness towards each other while the attractive co-worker at the office covers the wounded spouse with kind gestures all day. Even if it's just part of the job description such as typing letters, running errands, and making appointments, the wounded spouse might begin to desire this kind person in a sexual way because kindness feels good to the soul. Subconsciously the spouse is wondering what other ways this co-worker can make him feel good. It happens every day.

Protect your marriage with the bond of kindness!!

There's a song called the *Basics of Life* that says, "We need to get back to the basics of life: a heart that is pure and a love that is kind…." Love IS kind. And there is power in kindness.

The ancient Proverbs speaks of kindness:

> *"A man who is kind benefits himself, but a cruel man hurts himself."* (ESV)
>
> **Proverbs 11:17**

> *"What is desirable in a man is his kindness…"* (NASB)
>
> **Proverbs 19:22**

What spouse does not want to be desirable? We ALL hope to be desired by our spouses, and maybe we didn't realize how simple it is to BECOME desirable. Believe it or not, it doesn't take breast implants, losing weight, or more money to become desirable. I know of some happy, overweight, underpaid couples that have GREAT sex lives because they are kind to each other and make it a priority. It's really that simple.

Try it.

Then prepare your oils. Sometimes sex just happens. You're both asleep; a tossed leg lands on a slumbering spouse, then a hand. Then the sleepy couple wakes, the quiet stillness of the house stirs the linked pair, and both realize this is the perfect moment.

The. Perfect. Moment.

This is not the time to hop up and start mixing oils! NO! Have what you want right next to the bed at all times! Dry sex is for desert animals, not humans. Be ready. But avoid the mistake I made one time. Oils lay everywhere in our house, so finding one is never the problem. Finding the right one has proven to be the challenge! One night when the lights were out I reached for Mister and V6, I instead grabbed Thieves and OrthoEase! (FIRE!!!!!!!) I have a whole new definition for hot buns. Holy cow! Don't keep your hot oils on the night stand.

* If bad breath is an issue that would keep you from being intimate in the middle of the night, then put Thieves mouthwash in a small 2oz spray bottle and place it on your nightstand. One or two squirts in the mouth and voila...no more dragon's breath, and you did not have to get up and brush!

Show Me You Love Me

My husband is a type A, sharp, to the point kind of a guy. That's one reason he's a successful business owner, and it's one of the characteristics that attracted my attention when we first met. But that same quality can rub the wrong way occasionally and sometimes his words feel abrupt against my spirit. So we had a heart-to-heart one day when I was feeling rather pitiful and wounded. I told him I need him to SHOW me he loves me in little ways. I need him to SHOW me I'm his choice and will always be his choice! Here's my shortlist. (Don't judge me. Estrogen flows through my veins!)

1. I need a hug and kiss each morning before he leaves for work.

2. I NEED a kiss hello AFTER work. (I know! I'm so high maintenance with all this kissing!)

3. I like him to sit by ME during church! We used to sit with ALL our kids between us for crowd control, but I decided I like to hold his hand or lean on him during the sermon. It's like a mini date at the movies, only there's preaching and the lights are on. (I know it's a stretch, but with 11 kids, I take what I can get!) It's a small request that makes a HUGE difference at night when the lights click off.

4. My man is very task oriented with never-ending projects. So, many years ago, I told him it's important to me that he pauses work and sits at the head of the table during dinner, engaging with the kids as they each give their highs and lows for the day. He loves this time with the family, but he needed a little nudging to find out how sweet the intentional time together could be.

5. I need a weekly date. Just him and me. Over food at a restaurant. No phones. No kids. Scheduled. On the calendar. We settled on Saturday morning breakfast before the house is roaring with activity. It's nice. Makes me happy.

6. I prefer sex during the night versus during the day. It's certainly not a hard and fast rule but a personal preference for two reasons. First, my body feels best if I can stay off my feet after sex. This was more true during my child bearing years than now, but when it was true...it was VERY TRUE. I've noticed that I'm not bothered as much now that a few years have passed since our last child was born, but it was the case for a very long time. This is common for many childbearing women because during pregnancy, blood volume doubles, blood vessels expand, then the baby exits out the same place it entered, but 8lbs heavier. Everything returns to normal, (one of God's great miracles!) but somehow sex at night still feels best during the childbearing years. So for you women who feel pain after morning sex, just tell your husband that a friend who has 11 children told you it won't always be this way!

He'll be happy about that! You'll be able to have morning sex when your body isn't so busy carrying babies and giving birth.

The second reason is obvious. I feel prettier when I know he can't CLEARLY see my flaws! Now I know I'm contradicting my charge to you earlier to let your husband enjoy your naked body. I let mine enjoy my naked body. He can have a dim night light. ;)

My husband enjoys everything about my (high maintenance) list just as much as I do!! It's benefited both of us AND our children!

His list for me looks like this:

1. Have oatmeal ready for him each morning before work. (Otherwise, he buys donuts and feels like trash the rest of the day!)

2. Be willing to get naked often.

And... Well... that's about it! Thus the difference between men and women. They need food and sex, and *we have a list!*

Let's Get Naked!

Let's get naked; passionately love me, but don't lust me. The difference between love and lust must be addressed before clothes start flying. Love is so much richer than lust. Love satisfies. Love gives. Love cherishes. Love puts the desires of the other first. Love forgives. Love waits. Love protects. Love never fails. Love covers a multitude of sins. Love binds a marriage together. Love makes great sex!

Pure lust, however, is different from passionate love. Lust hurries. Lust pushes. Lust steals. Lust fumes. Lust wanders. Lust tears down. Lust begrudges. Lust destroys. Lust provokes. Lust always wants more. Lust has no place in the bedroom. Lust leaves one empty.

Passionate sex filled with love between a husband and wife satisfies beyond the moment. And isn't that what everyone is seeking? Rich contentment in life? Passionate love waters the soul of a married couple. Said another way, the physical satisfaction of passionate love pours over and waters the soul of a married couple. Not to mention it's pleasing to the One who created it. It makes God smile! :) However, passionate sex driven by lust without love may feel good physically in the moment, but it leaves both participants empty, even lonely. Which do you want? Complete satisfaction and oneness with your man, or fleeting pleasure and loneliness? Think about it.

I realize that lust is probably more of an issue for your husband than you, but you can show your husband how love feels. Show him passionate love when you touch him the way he wants to be touched. If he is the one always pursuing and you're not actively hungry for him and willing to explore unexplored territories, he will be left wanting. There are more than two positions for sex, friends, and many different places to kiss. Make sure you're exploring new territory. Consider that your husband is wired differently in his desires. Put his desires before yours, and you will find yourself satisfied, too. Your actions will show him love, and he will in turn want to please you. It's a beautiful circle. You take the initiative to stir the love in your marriage. Don't wait for him to begin first.

Besides showing him how to love you, help him rise to the occasion by speaking things to him as though they were. For instance, tell him you love his body even though it's not exactly the same body you married. You're wanting the same grace, remember? Whisper to him that he makes you the happiest girl in the world...and he will strive to live up to that. Utter edifying words that make him stand up straighter. You've probably heard the scripture, "The wise woman builds her house, but with her own hands the foolish one tears hers down." Proverbs 14:1 (NIV) Be a wise woman and build the house of your marriage with the words you speak about and to your husband, and show him love by the way you interact with him naked.

Now for the Magic Potions:

Ok, they are not really MAGIC potions, but they certainly enhance!! I can confidently say that when emotional intimacy is present between a husband and wife, adding these therapeutic essential oils CAN be magic! In my opinion, the mystery of how a husband and wife fit together so perfectly with little feel good happy spots in place is a supernatural - above and beyond magic - gift from God. So these recipes just make sex super duper, supernatural amazing like magic! *Got it?*

Are you ready for the magic? I mean recipes. Let's go!

Just Plain Silk - V-6

V-6 is a basic enhanced vegetable oil complex massage oil. It's known as a carrier oil, meaning it's the base you'll drop essential oils into in order to stretch an oil or dilute its temperature. You can use this plain and experience a silky massage or add the recommendations below to engage more of your senses.

If you struggle with dryness, V-6 (and the other massage oils listed below) will be your best friend. Another fun tip concerning V-6 is that if your husband's bodily fluid grosses you out, this masks it. Without lubricant, his secretion can feel sticky and taste salty. I understand this makes some women gag. First, let me encourage you to say to yourself, "I think I can, I think I can," con-

cerning getting over your abhorrence of it. It's part of sex. Get over it. I know that sounds harsh, but if you are going to be married for more than a few decades ('til death do us part!), you and your husband will have sex SEVERAL THOUSAND times!! Let's do the math. It's actually a fun exercise.

Drum roll please: If you have had sex 3 times a week for 10 years, you and your husband have been together 1,560 times!! Keep multiplying! Hopefully you will be married to your husband for more than 50 years. But let's just say you do the math on your 50th wedding anniversary. If you take an average of 3 times a week, you will have had sex 7,800! Look at all those opportunities you will have to explore each other. Find out the secret spots that melt your spouse. Realize that you're on a private journey with your man, and this part of your relationship should be planned, exciting, comfortable, spontaneous, forgiving, giving, generous, bold and above all...A PRIORITY.

Now back to the subject at hand, the best lubricant in the world. Be sure to cover his man parts with plenty of massage oil to make his secretions silky and to mask the taste. When you are adding essential oils, you will typically blend 1 drop essential oil in 1-8 tsp of V-6. For topical applications, apply 15-30 drops of essential oils to 1/8-1/4 cup V-6. The ratio depends on your personal preference, but who really measures in the middle of sex? Really! Be liberal! This stuff is safe! Use it freely! So in summary, V-6 is your basic carrier oil that doubles as a lubricant and masks the texture, taste and smell of bodily secretions that may bother you.

Great Balls of Fire! - Peppermint

Peppermint is stimulating! It awakens ALL your senses. Sex is a hot and sweaty sport, and peppermint cools the body down. I told a close friend how much fun my husband and I were having in the bedroom with my discovery of peppermint, but it was a short conversation and I didn't give her the rest of the story! She missed the part that peppermint should be diluted with a carrier oil such as V-6! She and her husband used it NEAT or undiluted, and she told me he was dancing around the room singing, "GREAT BALLS OF FIRE!" LOL...I felt terrible... hee hee!! Peppermint is COOL and HOT! But when diluted, it's just right. Peppermint also keeps the breath nice and fresh, which is impor-tant, since the mouth is a key player.

- 4 oz V-6

- 10 drops of peppermint

Mix well in small glass or stainless steel container.

- Aids in digestion
- Nausea
- Morning sickness
- Cramps of the upper gastrointestinal tract and bile ducts
- Helps dissipate gas
- Colds
- Coughs
- Inflammation of the mouth and throat
- Sinus and respiratory relief
- Mental focus

Did His Drive Dive? - Idaho Blue Spruce & Copaiba

A low sex drive in a husband can usually be overcome when the right steps are taken. If you know your husband needs a hormone boost, then this is definitely a combination you'll want to experiment with! It will fuel him with the male energy he needs to fulfill all his manly roles, without dangerous side effects. Every night before bed, put 8 drops each Idaho Blue Spruce and Copaiba on the soles of his feet. During sex, apply the mix below liberally directly on his man parts. If this is a problem for you because of the feeling of wiry hair, buy your husband an extra razor and the Shutran Shaving Cream. Tell him you'll both be extra happy if he'll mow his lawn, so to speak. And you will both enjoy the added sensitivity and stimulation if you do the same for him. Shaving, Brazilian wax and laser hair removal are all great options to bring you two even closer during sex and increase the fun! Give them all a try to see which option works for you!

- 2 oz V-6

- 15 drops Idaho Blue Spruce

- 15 drops Copaiba

Mix in glass or stainless steel container. Enjoy!

- Nerve Pain & Nerve Regeneration
- Increase energy level (Male/Female)
- Post Nasal Drip
- Sexual Pleasure
- Spinal Column Regeneration
- Weight Loss

- Cicatrizant – promotes healing of injuries by faster formation of scar or scab
- Assists in cleaning out wounds, scrapes etc to prevent any infection by pathogens
- Emollient – fancy word for moisturizes
- Astringent – shrinks skin tissue (which can have cosmetic benefits)
- Expectorant – aids in expelling phlegm
- Hypotensive – aid in lowering down blood pressure
- Calming

Let's do this! Wait! What just happened? - Lavender

Lavender is the perfect oil for young honeymooners. It's warm and soothing! It's the perfect choice for the wife who chills easily without covers. Because Young Living's lavender vitality is thera-peutic, it's safe to take internally (read: safe for licking 😋) and actually offers health benefits including its ability to eliminate nervous tension, relieve pain, enhance blood circulation and treat respiratory problems. Can you imagine getting all those benefits while you're having sex? When diluted with a carrier oil like V-6 oil, the floral taste is nice. A little side note: Young Living's other lavender without the vitality label came from the same farm, same plants, same factory. Nothing is added to it. It's straight lavender like the one labeled vitality. Do you think they are both safe for internal usage? Yeah, me too.

But here's a lavender warning!!!! Sex changes for some men after the 40th birthday. Lavender is so calming and relaxing that if you have BIG plans, there's a possibility that *ain't nothin' gonna work right for your husband,* and it could mess up your fun! Experiment with the knowledge that lavender is a relaxing oil. Drinking a few drops before sex might be ideal for a newlywed wife, but the old-er husband will most definitely want to avoid this one.

- 4 oz V-6 or coconut oil
- 10-20 drops lavender

•Muscular aches and pains: Use massage or muscle balm and oil
•Headaches: Massage into temples or use pulse point oil
•Aids in sleep: Use a drop of oil on pillow, sleep balm or drink
•Insect bites and stings: Use lavender oil on affected areas
•Soothes skin: Rub lavender into affected areas
•Burns, scalds and sunburn: Rub lavender into affected areas
•Calms irritability: Use bath salts with oil, massage oil
•Soothes hair and scalp
•Calms menstrual pain
•Room fragrance: Use lavender as an air freshener spray or in diffuser
•Cleanses wounds

Mix well in a glass container. Or just drop directly on your spouse!

Check Out That Monument - Goldenrod

The name of this oil makes me blush. Let's just say it lives up to its name. If erectile dysfunction is an issue for your husband, then rub goldenrod on the soles of his feet or on his man parts each night before bed. Goldenrod helps with blood flow in the body, which happens to benefit his manly functions. The smell of goldenrod is hmmm...unusual, so use this opportunity to add some other manly oils to make a blend. Then apply to your man's feet nightly. Mister and/or Shutran would be a nice addition to goldenrod and, of course, V6 massage oil. It may take a few weeks or so for your husband to notice a difference, but then again he may notice the first night. You won't know until you try. This oil could be a game changer in your bedroom.

- Promotes blood flow
- Increases libido
- Relaxing
- Supports healthy kidneys
- Supports healthy bladder
- Nicknamed "Liberty Tea" by the Pilgrims

Turn Up the Music! The Kids are Awake! - Ylang Ylang

Bring on the fun! The smell of Ylang Ylang is bewitching. It calms nerves immediately, which is a MUST if the wife is going to engage!! If you are an ounce like me, you KNOW it's quite a feat to unwind quickly after a long, frenzied day as a busy momma! It's hard to switch roles from (sweet mommy voice to the children) "Mommy's here! Let me help you!" to (sultry sexy voice to your husband) "Hot Momma's here. Let me kiss you!" Know what I mean? Sheesh! But if there was an on switch, it might be Ylang Ylang. Diffuse in the room at least 20 minutes before your husband joins you. Rub on your neck, wrists, and ankles, and let him find the smell. Enchanting!!

- Alleviates mental tension
- Aphrodisiac
- Balancing effect in the body
- Boosts hair development when massaged into scalp
- Commonly used as a perfume

Want to play, Mister?

Mister essential oil blend promotes male hormone balance, stimulates and balances functions of the prostate, and reduces mental fatigue. This one gives both my husband and me a strong, confident energy...not like caffeine, but rather a youthful vigor. It supports testosterone which is usually needed around the 40th birthday. We love the smell and the way it makes us feel. Apply like a cologne during the day. You can use it with V-6 for an all over the body massage, too.

- 1 tsp of V-6

- 15 drops of Mister

Mix well. Enjoy!

- Balances male and female energy
- Supports overall emotional and mental wellbeing
- Best for men 30-years-old and up

Ooh La La - Lady Sclareol

This oil blend will help the reluctant lover warm up her hormones. The oils in this blend are Geranium, Coriander, Vetiver, Orange, Clary, Bergamot, Ylang Ylang, Royal Hawaiian Sandalwood, Spanish Sage, Jasmine, Idaho Blue Spruce, Spearmint, and Hinoki. If you do a little research on the oils in this blend, you will quickly see why it's such a GREAT choice for the wife. Wear this one like perfume NEAT or use directly on private parts NEAT for awakening. The carrier oil is optional.

- 2 oz V-6

- 25 drops of Lady Sclareol

- 10 Ylang Ylang

- Mix well on your own or your husband's body or in a small glass or stainless steel container. Enjoy!

- Emotionally balancing
- May help soothe mild mood changes
- May help alleviate cramps associated with menstrual cycle
- Aphrodisiac, love, romantic intimacy, sexual energy

Turn Down the Lights! - Sensation oil

Sensation essential oil blend has a soft, romantic aroma. Its blend is a combination of Ylang-ylang, Geranium, Coriander, Bergamot and Jasmine. But Sensation oil is so much more than a sensuous smell. It offers health benefits that will keep you coming back for more! The therapeutic properties in Sensation oil support the skin, which makes it perfect for sex in any stage of life. Thinning skin is part of the aging process (50's, 60's, 70's, 80's), which can make sex painful. If this is the case, enjoy both the aroma and benefits of Sensation oil.

- Use NEAT or 2 oz V-6

- 15 drops Sensation oil

Mix well in glass or stainless steel container. Enjoy!

- Promotes feelings of love and romance
- Uplifting and refreshing
- Supports healthy skin

Sex in the Forest! - Balsam Fir

If you're married to a hunter who would live outdoors if he could and sex in the forest is his fantasy, then this is the oil for you. Balsam Fir has a woodsy, manly smell that can be enjoyed right on top of your sheets. The aroma will whisk your husband's mind into the forest, but your bare body will remain safe on the comfort of your sheets, away from pine needles and outdoor pests. You and your husband will find the aroma both grounding and balancing- relaxing to the body, yet stimulating to the mind.

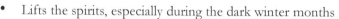

- Lifts the spirits, especially during the dark winter months
- Powerful chest decongestant
- Stimulates the circulatory system
- Soothes pain in muscles and joints
- Supports healthy immune functioning
- Relieves achy joints
- Removes fluid from joints
- Eases back pain
- Transforms negative energy and thoughts

Man!! - Shutran

This is a personal favorite. And my husband knows it, which I LOVE! Shutran is balancing for both men and women, but smells more like a MAN to me! Have your husband apply it like cologne. You will both benefit! This is one you seriously need to experience! The Shutran blend comes in oil, shaving cream and an aftershave lotion. It gives a man confidence and makes a wife want to cling to him.

- Promotes feelings of vitality and energy
- Enhances feelings of vigor and masculinity
- Boosts confidence
- Proprietary essential oil blend formulated especially for man (but women may benefit from it too)

Shortcuts to Gourmet Fun!

I'm all about shortcuts concerning...well...EVERYTHING!! The following recipes are shortcuts to fun in the bedroom because these massage oils are already infused with essential oils, so you don't have to measure or count drops. You CAN do a little tweaking simply for personal preference or other objectives like libido stimulation, but the massage oils are great to use as is.

Be a Hottie! – Ortho Sport

 Silky and penetrating!! It's infused with Wintergreen, Peppermint, Thyme, and Oregano. YL created it for muscle massages, not necessarily for private parts, but since the oils in this blend feel stimulating, smell invigorating, and penetrate deep, you may enjoy this one intimately. It's hot. Fair skinned people with sensitive skin may experience as hot/hot. So BE SURE to dilute this blend in half or more V-6 the first time you use it.

- Half V-6
- Half OrthoSport

Mix well in container of choice. Enjoy!

Mmmmmm – Ortho Ease

Here's another fun blend. This infused oil is minty, invigorating and provides a tantalizing experience! The ingredients in this one are Wintergreen, Peppermint, Juniper, and Marjoram. If you choose to dilute, do the following:

- Half Ortho Ease

- Half V-6

Mix well in container of choice. Enjoy!

Sex at the Spa - Relaxation Oil

This one has a spa feel. The ingredients are Lavender, Tangerine, Coriander, and Spearmint. This combination helps a couple unwind after a busy day! Not too hot. Not too cool. Just right. This one is fun to use when your activity is in a steamy shower.

The King - Sensation Massage Oil

No! That is not a typo. Sensation Massage Oil and Sensation essential oil are two different products. This massage oil was created for love. Some have called it exhilarating! The ingredients that set this one apart are Ylang Ylang, Jasmine, and Geranium, but it's loaded with several others!

No need to dilute this one. Just Enjoy!

Exotic Linen Spray

Do you want a sexy atmosphere floating around your room? Diffuse 4 drops each for at least 20 minutes before you lock the door. Or make a room spray with the following:

24 drops essential oils (8 drops each of Ylang Ylang, Sensation oil, Rose oil)

- 1 oz. vodka

- 1 oz. purified water

- 2 oz. glass spray bottle

Mix in a 2 oz dark glass bottle.

Shake well. Spray liberally on linens to set the mood.

In Closing

It's time for you to start playing with oils in the bedroom with your husband. Tell him you want to have more sex, but you need these essential oils for your experiments with him! I bet he won't argue with you. Enjoy every aspect of your husband's body as you delve into this new world of marital intimacy with therapeutic essential oils. Turn up the passionate love with your spouse! Be brave, and try new things! Tell him you want to experiment to see what works for you, and know it's okay to find some things that aren't your favorite. ! And by all means... *have FUN!*

Sincerely,

Terri

Get Started with the Oils

Thank you for giving me your time. If a friend has been telling you about Young Living's amazing oils, QUICKLY go tell her you're READY to buy! If not, then I would be HONORED to help you on your journey into an oil-infused lifestyle! Young Living offers an expansive list of essential oil products that can benefit your family from the kitchen to the bedroom. From health supplements to cleaning products, Young Living's offerings are natural, effective and infused with therapeutic-grade essential oils that you will LOVE!

Check out our website for more education: justalittledrop.com

Many Blessings to you and your spouse,

Terri Bonin

Young Living Independent Distributor

#892602

Recommended Reading List

14 Days to Ignite Your Marriage by Terri Bonin

The Act of Marriage: The Beauty of Sexual Love by Tim LaHaye and Beverly LaHaye

Sheet Music: Uncovering the Secrets of Sexual Intimacy in Marriage by Kevin Leman

Intended for Pleasure: Sex Technique and Sexual Fulfillment in Christian Marriage by Ed M.D. Wheat and Gaye Wheat

Love Your Husband/Love Yourself: Embracing God's Purpose for Passion in Marriage by Jennifer Flanders

31 Days to Great Sex by Sheila Wray Gregoire

Hot, Holy, and Humorous: Sex in Marriage by God's Design by J. Parker.

Love and Respect: The Love She Most Desires: The Respect He Desperately Needs by Emerson Eggerichs

Other Books by the Author

14 Days to Ignite Your Marriage

31 Days to Fit

Live, Love, Laugh and Laundry?

Fat Proof Your Kids

A Fat Proof Meal Plan (Fat Proof Your Kids Book 2)

Drops of Pleasure

by Terri Bonin

Conroe, TX

www.JustaLittleDrop.com

Cover by Angela Rose